THE JPS B'NAI MITZVAH TORAH COMMENTARY

Be-midbar (Numbers 1:1–4:20)
Haftarah (Hosea 2:1–22)

Rabbi Jeffrey K. Salkin

The Jewish Publication Society · Philadelphia
University of Nebraska Press · Lincoln

© 2018 by Rabbi Jeffrey K. Salkin. All rights reserved.
Published by The University of Nebraska Press as a
Jewish Publication Society book.
Manufactured in the United States of America
♾

INTRODUCTION

News flash: the most important thing about becoming bar or bat mitzvah isn't the party. Nor is it the presents. Nor even being able to celebrate with your family and friends—as wonderful as those things are. Nor is it even standing before the congregation and reading the prayers of the liturgy—as important as that is.

No, the most important thing about becoming bar or bat mitzvah is sharing Torah with the congregation. And why is that? Because of all Jewish skills, that is the most important one.

Here is what is true about rites of passage: you can tell what a culture values by the tasks it asks its young people to perform on their way to maturity. In American culture, you become responsible for driving, responsible for voting, and yes, responsible for drinking responsibly.

In some cultures, the rite of passage toward maturity includes some kind of trial, or a test of strength. Sometimes, it is a kind of "outward bound" camping adventure. Among the Maasai tribe in Africa, it is traditional for a young person to hunt and kill a lion. In some Hispanic cultures, fifteen year-old girls celebrate the *quinceañera*, which marks their entrance into maturity.

What is Judaism's way of marking maturity? It combines both of these rites of passage: *responsibility* and *test*. You show that you are on your way to becoming a *responsible* Jewish adult through a public *test* of strength and knowledge—reading or chanting Torah, and then teaching it to the congregation.

This is the most important Jewish ritual mitzvah (commandment), and that is how you demonstrate that you are, truly, bar or bat mitzvah—old enough to be responsible for the mitzvot.

What Is Torah?

So, what exactly is the Torah? You probably know this already, but let's review.

The Torah (teaching) consists of "the five books of Moses," sometimes also called the *chumash* (from the Hebrew word *chameish,* which means "five"), or, sometimes, the Greek word Pentateuch (which means "the five teachings").

Here are the five books of the Torah, with their common names and their Hebrew names.

> **Genesis (The beginning), which in Hebrew is Bere'shit (from the first words—"When God began to create").** Bere'shit spans the years from Creation to Joseph's death in Egypt. Many of the Bible's best stories are in Genesis: the creation story itself; Adam and Eve in the Garden of Eden; Cain and Abel; Noah and the Flood; and the tales of the Patriarchs and Matriarchs, Abraham, Isaac, Jacob, Sarah, Rebekah, Rachel, and Leah. It also includes one of the greatest pieces of world literature, the story of Joseph, which is actually the oldest complete novel in history, comprising more than one-quarter of all Genesis.

> **Exodus (Getting out), which in Hebrew is Shemot (These are the names).** Exodus begins with the story of the Israelite slavery in Egypt. It then moves to the rise of Moses as a leader, and the Israelites' liberation from slavery. After the Israelites leave Egypt, they experience the miracle of the parting of the Sea of Reeds (or "Red Sea"); the giving of the Ten Commandments at Mount Sinai; the idolatry of the Golden Calf; and the design and construction of the Tabernacle and of the ark for the original tablets of the law, which our ancestors carried with them in the desert. Exodus also includes various ethical and civil laws, such as "You shall not wrong a stranger or oppress him, for you were strangers in the land of Egypt" (22:20).

> **Leviticus (about the Levites), or, in Hebrew, Va-yikra' (And God called).** It goes into great detail about the kinds of sacrifices that the ancient Israelites brought as offerings; the laws of ritual purity; the animals that were permitted and forbidden for eating (the beginnings of the tradition of kashrut, the Jewish dietary laws); the diagnosis of various skin diseases; the ethical laws of holiness; the ritual calendar of the Jewish year; and various agricultural laws concerning the treatment of the Land of Israel. Leviticus is basically the manual of ancient Judaism.

> Numbers (because the book begins with the census of the Israelites), or, in Hebrew, Be-midbar (In the wilderness). The book describes the forty years of wandering in the wilderness and the various rebellions against Moses. The constant theme: "Egypt wasn't so bad. Maybe we should go back." The greatest rebellion against Moses was the negative reports of the spies about the Land of Israel, which discouraged the Israelites from wanting to move forward into the land. For that reason, the "wilderness generation" must die off before a new generation can come into maturity and finish the journey.

> Deuteronomy (The repetition of the laws of the Torah), or, in Hebrew, Devarim (The words). The final book of the Torah is, essentially, Moses's farewell address to the Israelites as they prepare to enter the Land of Israel. Here we find various laws that had been previously taught, though sometimes with different wording. Much of Deuteronomy contains laws that will be important to the Israelites as they enter the Land of Israel—laws concerning the establishment of a monarchy and the ethics of warfare. Perhaps the most famous passage from Deuteronomy contains the *Shema,* the declaration of God's unity and uniqueness, and the *Ve-ahavta,* which follows it. Deuteronomy ends with the death of Moses on Mount Nebo as he looks across the Jordan Valley into the land that he will not enter.

Jews read the Torah in sequence—starting with Bere'shit right after Simchat Torah in the autumn, and then finishing Devarim on the following Simchat Torah. Each Torah portion is called a parashah (division; sometimes called a *sidrah,* a place in the order of the Torah reading). The stories go around in a full circle, reminding us that we can always gain more insights and more wisdom from the Torah. This means that if you don't "get" the meaning this year, don't worry—it will come around again.

And What Else? The Haftarah

We read or chant the Torah from the Torah scroll—the most sacred thing that a Jewish community has in its possession. The Torah is written without vowels, and the ability to read it and chant it is part of the challenge and the test.

But there is more to the synagogue reading. Every Torah reading has an accompanying haftarah reading. Haftarah means "conclusion," because there was once a time when the service actually ended with that reading. Some scholars believe that the reading of the haftarah originated at a time when non-Jewish authorities outlawed the reading of the Torah, and the Jews read the haftarah sections instead. In fact, in some synagogues, young people who become bar or bat mitzvah read very little Torah and instead read the entire haftarah portion.

The haftarah portion comes from the Nevi'im, the prophetic books, which are the second part of the Jewish Bible. It is either read or chanted from a Hebrew Bible, or maybe from a booklet or a photocopy.

The ancient sages chose the haftarah passages because their themes reminded them of the words or stories in the Torah text. Sometimes, they chose *haftarah* with special themes in honor of a festival or an upcoming festival.

Not all books in the prophetic section of the Hebrew Bible consist of prophecy. Several are historical. For example:

The book of Joshua tells the story of the conquest and settlement of Israel.

The book of Judges speaks of the period of early tribal rulers who would rise to power, usually for the purpose of uniting the tribes in war against their enemies. Some of these leaders are famous: Deborah, the great prophetess and military leader, and Samson, the biblical strong man.

The books of Samuel start with Samuel, the last judge, and then move to the creation of the Israelite monarchy under Saul and David (approximately 1000 BCE).

The books of Kings tell of the death of King David, the rise of King Solomon, and how the Israelite kingdom split into the Northern Kingdom of Israel and the Southern Kingdom of Judah (approximately 900 BCE).

And then there are the books of the prophets, those spokesmen for God whose words fired the Jewish conscience. Their names are immortal: Isaiah, Jeremiah, Ezekiel, Amos, Hosea, among others.

Someone once said: "There is no evidence of a biblical prophet ever being invited back a second time for dinner." Why? Because the prophets were tough. They had no patience for injustice, apathy, or hypocrisy. No one escaped their criticisms. Here's what they taught:

> God commands the Jews to behave decently toward one another. In fact, God cares more about basic ethics and decency than about ritual behavior.
> God chose the Jews *not* for special privileges, but for special duties to humanity.
> As bad as the Jews sometimes were, there was always the possibility that they would improve their behavior.
> As bad as things might be now, it will not always be that way. Someday, there will be universal justice and peace. Human history is moving forward toward an ultimate conclusion that some call the Messianic Age: a time of universal peace and prosperity for the Jewish people and for all the people of the world.

Your Mission—To Teach Torah to the Congregation

On the day when you become bar or bat mitzvah, you will be reading, or chanting, Torah—in Hebrew. You will be reading, or chanting, the haftarah—in Hebrew. That is the major skill that publicly marks the becoming of bar or bat mitzvah. But, perhaps even more important than that, you need to be able to teach something about the Torah portion, and perhaps the haftarah as well.

And that is where this book comes in. It will be a very valuable resource for you, and your family, in the b'nai mitzvah process.

Here is what you will find in it:

> A brief **summary** of every Torah portion. This is a basic overview of the portion; and, while it might not refer to everything in the Torah portion, it will explain its most important aspects.
> A list of the **major ideas** in the Torah portion. The purpose: to make the Torah portion real, in ways that we can relate to. Every Torah portion contains unique ideas, and when you put all

of those ideas together, you actually come up with a list of Judaism's most important ideas.

> Two ***divrei Torah*** ("words of Torah," or "sermonettes") for each portion. These *divrei Torah* explain significant aspects of the Torah portion in accessible, reader-friendly language. Each *devar Torah* contains references to **traditional** Jewish sources (those that were written before the modern era), as well as **modern** sources and quotes. We have searched, far and wide, to find sources that are unusual, interesting, and not just the "same old stuff" that many people already know about the Torah portion. Why did we include these minisermons in the volume? Not because we want you to simply copy those sermons and pass them off as your own (that would be cheating), though you are free to quote from them. We included them so that you can see what is possible—how you can try to make meaning for yourself out of the words of Torah.

> **Connections:** This is perhaps the most valuable part. It's a list of questions that you can ask yourself, or that others might help you think about—any of which can lead to the creation of your *devar Torah.*

Note: you don't have to like everything that's in a particular Torah portion. Some aren't that loveable. Some are hard to understand; some are about religious practices that people today might find confusing, and even offensive; some contain ideas that we might find totally outmoded.

But this doesn't have to get in the way. After all, most kids spend a lot of time thinking about stories that contain ideas that modern people would find totally bizarre. Any good medieval fantasy story falls into that category.

And we also believe that, if you spend just a little bit of time with those texts, you can begin to understand what the author was trying to say.

This volume goes one step further. Sometimes, the haftarah comes off as a second thought, and no one really thinks about it. We have tried to solve that problem by including a **summary** of each haftarah, and then a mini-sermon on the haftarah. This will help you learn how these sacred words are relevant to today's world, and even to your own life.

All Bible quotations come from the NJPS translation, which is found in the many different editions of the JPS TANAKH; in the Conservative movement's *Etz Hayim: Torah and Commentary;* in the Reform movement's *Torah: A Modern Commentary;* and in other Bible commentaries and study guides.

How Do I Write a *Devar Torah*?

It really is easier than it looks.

There are many ways of thinking about the *devar Torah*. It is, of course, a short sermon on the meaning of the Torah (and, perhaps, the haftarah) portion. It might even be helpful to think of the *devar Torah* as a "book report" on the portion itself.

The most important thing you can know about this sacred task is: *Learn* the words. *Love* the words. Teach people what it could mean to *live* the words.

Here's a basic outline for a *devar Torah:*

"My Torah portion is (name of portion) _____,
   from the book of _____, chapter

_____.

"In my Torah portion, we learn that_____
   (Summary of portion)
"For me, the most important lesson of this Torah portion is (what
   is the best thing in the portion? Take the portion as a whole;
   your *devar Torah* does not have to be only, or specifically, on the
   verses that you are reading).
"As I learned my Torah portion, I found myself wondering:
   ‣ *Raise a question that the Torah portion itself raises.*
   ‣ *"Pick a fight"* with the portion. Argue with it.
   ‣ *Answer a question* that is listed in the "Connections" section of
      each Torah portion.
   ‣ *Suggest a question to your rabbi* that you would want the rabbi
      to answer in his or her own *devar Torah* or sermon.

"I have lived the values of the Torah by _____
(here, you can talk about how the Torah portion relates to your
own life. If you have done a mitzvah project, you can talk about
that here).

How To Keep It from Being Boring
(and You from Being Bored)

Some people just don't like giving traditional speeches. From our per-
spective, that's really okay. Perhaps you can teach Torah in a different
way—one that makes sense to you.

> * Write an "open letter" to one of the characters in your Torah por-
>   tion. "Dear Abraham: I hope that your trip to Canaan was not too
>   hard . . ." "Dear Moses: Were you afraid when you got the Ten
>   Commandments on Mount Sinai? I sure would have been . . ."
> * Write a news story about what happens. Imagine yourself to
>   be a television or news reporter. "Residents of neighboring cit-
>   ies were horrified yesterday as the wicked cities of Sodom and
>   Gomorrah were burned to the ground. Some say that God was
>   responsible . . ."
> * Write an imaginary interview with a character in your Torah portion.
> * Tell the story from the point of view of another character, or a mi-
>   nor character, in the story. For instance, tell the story of the Gar-
>   den of Eden from the point of view of the serpent. Or the story
>   of the Binding of Isaac from the point of view of the ram, which
>   was substituted for Isaac as a sacrifice. Or perhaps the story of
>   the sale of Joseph from the point of view of his coat, which was
>   stripped off him and dipped in a goat's blood.
> * Write a poem about your Torah portion.
> * Write a song about your Torah portion.
> * Write a play about your Torah portion, and have some friends act
>   it out with you.
> * Create a piece of artwork about your Torah portion.

The bottom line is: Make this a joyful experience. Yes—it could
even be fun.

The Very Last Thing You Need to Know at This Point

The Torah scroll is written without vowels. Why? Don't *sofrim* (Torah scribes) know the vowels?

Of course they do.

So, why do they leave the vowels out?

One reason is that the Torah came into existence at a time when sages were still arguing about the proper vowels, and the proper pronunciation.

But here is another reason: The Torah text, as we have it today, and as it sits in the scroll, is actually *an unfinished work*. Think of it: the words are just sitting there. Because they have no vowels, it is as if they have no voice.

When we read the Torah publicly, we give voice to the ancient words. And when we find meaning in those ancient words, and we talk about those meanings, those words jump to life. They enter our lives. They make our world deeper and better.

Mazal tov to you, and your family. This is your journey toward Jewish maturity. Love it.

THE TORAH

✣ Be-midbar: Numbers 1:1–4:20

We start a new book of the Torah: Numbers, which in Hebrew is Be-midbar (In the wilderness). The book gets its English name from the various censuses that are central to this Torah portion. Each census has a different purpose: to determine the number of able-bodied men available to serve as soldiers in a time of war; the number of Levites; and then, the numbers in a Levite subclan, the family of Kohath.

As the Israelites prepare to march into the wilderness, it becomes necessary to determine the positions of the various tribes as they carry the ark and the sacred vessels of the Tabernacle, the Tent of Meeting (*mishkan*).

Summary

> God commands Moses to take a census of all men over the age of twenty who are able to bear arms. The text lists the head of each tribe who will assist with the census, and then lists the population of each tribe. The total number of Israelites (or, more accurately, males over the age of twenty) is 603,550. (1:1–54)

> God gives Moses and Aaron the details of how the Israelite camp is to be arranged around the Tabernacle—on which side each tribe is to stand—along with the chieftain of the tribe and the number of troops in each tribe. (2:1–14)

> God commands Moses to take a census of the Levites, who will be responsible for taking care of the Tabernacle's vessels. The age limit is all males from the age of one month and older. The Levites serve in the place of all Israelite firstborn sons, which is the origin of the traditional ceremony of *pidyon ha-ben* (the redemption of the firstborn) when the child is thirty days old. The Torah then records the census of all the subclans of the Levites: Gershon, Kohath, and Merari—along with the specific duties of those clans. (3:5–39)

> The Kohath clan is assigned the most delicate, and perhaps the most dangerous, work of all. They are to carry the most sacred objects of the Tabernacle, and not by hand. Rather, they had to carry them on their shoulders. (4:1–20)

The Big Ideas

> **Every Jew "counts."** Wherever they have lived, Jews have always been a minority. That is one reason why it has been necessary for every Jew to do the best that he or she can to ensure the vitality of Jewish life. A Hasidic teacher, Levi Yitzchak of Berdichev, taught that there was the same number of Israelites—603,550—as there are letters in the Torah scroll. Just as the Torah scroll would be invalid if a letter were missing, if any Jew slacks off, Judaism itself loses energy.

> **The Tabernacle is at the center of the Israelite camp.** The purpose of the Jewish people is to be a holy people, a people centered around its tradition. The Tabernacle was like a portable version of Mount Sinai. The arrangement of the tribes around the Tabernacle is hardly random. A midrash says that the tribes stood around it in exactly the same pattern as their ancestors stood around Jacob's coffin when they carried him back to Israel for burial. In this way, we learn that Jews always carry their memories with them.

> **For a Levite, one month old is "old enough."** Whereas the age for fighting was twenty, the age for levitical duty—taking care of the Tabernacle—is only one month. What can a one-month-old child do to take care of the Tabernacle? Nothing. But this teaches us that Jewish education must begin when a child is very young. Our earliest memories and experiences help shape the kinds of people we will become.

> **Even the most "menial" tasks can be holy.** The Kohath clan, a subclan of the Levites, was responsible for carrying the holiest objects of the Tabernacle. They were not supposed to carry them by hand; rather, they had to carry them on their shoulders. This is an act of physical exertion. Jewish life requires many kinds of exertions—intellectual, spiritual, and physical.

Divrei Torah

DO YOU COUNT?

If you find this Torah portion somewhat tedious, you're not alone. Generations of Jews would probably agree with you. All those names of obscure people, all those numbers—it is about as exciting as reading the telephone book.

Contemporary Jews like to wonder aloud about how many Jews there really are, and what those numbers mean. They love to argue about who is a Jew, and how many Jews there are in different countries, and where Jews live, and what Jews do. You really can't blame them. After all, for a people that lost six million during the Shoah (Holocaust), numbers matter.

But in biblical times, what good was a census, anyway? And why does God tell Moses to count the Israelites? After all, doesn't God know everything, especially how many Israelites there are?

A medieval sage, Rabbi Isaac Arama, teaches that this was so Moses would know that each Israelite was not just part of the entire people, but that each one had individual worth. "They were all equal in stature, and yet the stature of each one was different." Every Jew has something precious inside of him or her. And if we take seriously the idea that the 603,550 Israelites in the census represent the traditional number of 603,550 letters in the Torah, we can interpret that to mean that every Jew has some Torah not only to learn, but also to teach.

Take another look at that number—603,550. Are those all the Israelites? No way. Think about who wasn't counted. Cantor Rachel Stock Spilker writes: "What about the woman who might have wished to fight? Or how about the 19-year-old man, just months short of his 20th birthday, eager to serve God and his people? How about the 23-year-old male who doesn't have the right number of limbs since one of his was lost in a childhood accident?"

This is always the problem with counting people: often some get omitted. That not only means that the count or the census is inaccurate; it means that people are left out, and they know it. It hurts. That is why the term for "counting" is *se'u rosh*—literally, "lift up the head."

The act of counting should lift people's heads, and help them feel that their lives and contributions have dignity and meaning.

That is why some people say that nowadays when we count Jews we should make sure that every Jew counts.

How are you making sure that your Jewish life counts?

WHO'S YOUR DADDY—REALLY?

Is there an omission in this Torah portion? Numbers 3 begins: "This is the line of Aaron and Moses at the time that the Lord spoke with Moses on Mount Sinai." And then, it goes on to list Aaron's sons—but not the sons of Moses. Why does it only list Aaron's sons? What ever happened to the sons of Moses?

Moses did have sons—Gershom and Eliezer. And they are famous for . . . nothing. They disappear from the story. Why? Perhaps it wants to make a very big point: Moses was not a king. It was not his intention, nor was it the Torah's intention, to have him create a dynasty. His sons are, well, just "normal" people.

Why then does it list Aaron's sons? Precisely because Moses was their teacher—Moshe Rabbeinu, "Moses, our rabbi," the master teacher of Israel. Rashi, the great medieval commentator, teaches us: "It lists only the sons of Aaron, but calls them 'the line of Moses'—because he taught them Torah. Teaching Torah to someone is like being their parent."

This reminds us that teaching is so important—that it is like parenting, and that parenting is a form of teaching. Indeed, the Hebrew word for "teacher" (*moreh*) and "parent" (*horeh*) are from the same root. And so is the word Torah! They all mean "instruction" or "teaching" in one form or another.

When Jews remember a departed father, it is traditional to refer to him as *avi mori*, "my father, my teacher." That is the greatest sign of respect, the highest compliment one can utter. The job of a Jewish parent is to be a teacher of Torah. And when people cannot have children, one way that they can be involved in nurturing young people is, in fact, to teach them. If you ask teachers how they feel about what they do, they might just tell you that, at times, they do feel as if they are parenting their students.

Look at all the family names in this Torah portion. The Torah is pretty obsessed with who your father is (much less, sadly, with who your mother is). People are often described as being *ben* . . . (the son of . . .). For the first thousand years of Judaism, during the biblical era, Jewish identity was in fact passed down by the father. (It changed in the Rabbinic period to the mother . . . that is another story.)

But, in later generations, Judaism became less concerned with "who's your daddy?" and more concerned with "who's your teacher?" That is why Rabbinic literature is filled with references to who taught what to whom, and the necessity of quoting your sources accurately (meaning, don't plagiarize! and give credit where credit is due). The ancient sages even said that if both your father and your teacher were taken captive (a sad reality in ancient times) and you only had enough money to ransom one of them the teacher gets priority.

The contemporary teacher Howard Eilberg-Schwartz teaches us: "Just as a son must perpetuate his father's lineage, a disciple must preserve his rabbi's teaching."

So, who are your teachers? What is their Torah? How are you furthering what they have taught you?

Connections

- Do you agree with the way that the census was carried out? Who was left out of the census?
- How do we make sure that every Jew counts? How does your Jewish life count?
- In what way will you make your "letter" of the Torah—your own piece of the Jewish heritage—come alive?
- In what ways are teachers and parents alike? How are they different?
- What are some of the most valuable life lessons that you have learned from your parents? From various teachers? Which lessons do you think you will remember in decades to come?

THE HAFTARAH

❖ Be-midbar: Hosea 2:1–22

The book of Numbers gets its English name from the fact that it begins with a census of the people. In Hebrew it is Be-midbar, "the book of the wilderness," because it's an account of the wilderness wanderings of the Israelites, as they make their way to the Land of Israel.

In the haftarah, the prophet Hosea relates to both themes (and this is the connection to the Torah portion). He tells the reader that there will come a time when the People of Israel will be as numerous as the "sands of the sea, which cannot be measured or counted." The prophet also refers to the *midbar*, the spiritual wilderness in which the Israelites will find themselves, due to their sinning.

God's Broken Heart

Let's admit it: this is tough stuff—perhaps the toughest haftarah in the entire cycle of the Jewish year. That's because Hosea uses such graphic language and is so critical of his people. But it's easier to understand if we can see just what is going on here. Hosea was a prophet who lived in the Northern Kingdom of Israel in the eighth century BCE. The biggest issue there was that the people were constantly forsaking God and worshiping the Canaanite god, Baal.

According to Hosea, Israel's actions were a major disappointment, and even an insult, to God. It was as if God had a wife (the People of Israel) who had other lovers; the People of Israel was committing adultery! Remember that the Israelites and God have pledged themselves to each other in a covenant going all the way back to Sinai. Like a marriage, that covenant was based on faithfulness. The Jewish theologian Abraham Joshua Heschel writes: "Idolatry is adultery. More than stupidity, it is lewdness. Israel is like a wanton wife; the Lord is like a faithful, loving but forsaken husband."

God wanted Hosea to understand these feelings of betrayal. So, in a radical move, God commanded Hosea to marry Gomer, a prostitute.

(Or maybe Hosea just thought he had to do something radical to dramatize his message.) Gomer ran around with other lovers, causing the prophet deep heartache. Then God said to Hosea: Perhaps you'll understand how I feel. Now perhaps you can convince the People of Israel to stop what they are doing and be loyal only to me.

That's where this haftarah comes in. God demands that the prophet send his wife away. According to the Talmud: "God said: 'I will order Hosea: "Go and marry a prostitute and have children with that prostitute." Then, I will order him: "Send her away!" If he will be able to send her away, I will send Israel away, too.'" This is amazing; God is depending on the prophet to help determine whether Israel will be sent away from divine favor: "let her put . . . her adultery from between her breasts. Else I will strip her naked and leave her as on the day she was born" (Hosea 2: 4–5).

If you see something sexist in the way God is acting, you are not alone. In those days, marriages were far from the kind of equal relationships that contemporary couples want. To quote Rabbi Lia Bass: "God has the authority of possession and control over Israel in the same way that a husband has authority over a wife. The people, by definition, are subservient to God's will. Women, therefore, should be subservient to men." While the aim of God and the prophet is worthy—a faithful relationship—the means to achieving it, by exploiting Hosea and Gomer, is questionable.

This haftarah, like other parts of the Bible, has ideas about God that we may find difficult to understand. God is not just a distant God; the supreme ruler God is actually emotionally vulnerable. God had to put the prophet Hosea through this terrible experience just so that the prophet could empathize with God's feelings.

God promises that there will be a renewed, intimate connection with the Jewish people. "I will espouse you forever" (2:21). These are beautiful words and a noble ideal. In fact, traditional Jews say these words as, each day, they put on tefillin, the leather straps wrapped on the arm and head as commanded in the Torah. The relationship of the people with God endures, with its ups and downs, just like in a marriage. Ideally it will be based on mutual trust and affection, not simply on God's power over the relationship. The medieval commentator Rashi says: "You will worship me from love, and not from fear."

A broken marriage—and other broken relationships—can lead to a broken heart. But if we do everything we can, maybe our ties with those we care about, and our hearts, will heal.

❖ Notes

CPSIA information can be obtained
at www.ICGtesting.com
Printed in the USA
LVHW032143171118
597514LV00005BA/393/P